Learning Guitar with Hymns

Lessons

Introduction 3
The Design of Your Guitar 4
Playing Position 6
The Structure of Guitar Music 8
The Notes 10
Notes on the First String 12
Notes on the Second String 14
Notes on the Third String 15
Notes on the Fourth String 17
The Chord "D" 19
Notes on the Fifth String 20
The Chord "C" 22
Notes on the Sixth string 23
The Chord "G" 24
Common Chords 25

Practice Sheets

Practice Sheets 26
"The design of your Guitar." 27
"Playing Position" 29
"The Structure of Guitar Music" 30
"The Notes" 32
"Notes on the First String" 33
"Notes on the second string" 36
"Notes on the Third String" 37
"Notes on the Fourth String" 38
"The Chord D" 40
"Notes on the Fifth String" 41
"The Chord C" 42
"Notes on the Sixth String" 43
"The Chord G" 44
"Common Chords" 45

Introduction

Welcome to the "Learning Guitar with Hymns" teaching series! This series of books is designed for the beginner guitarist who wants to learn guitar in a way that is detailed, yet simple and comprehensive.

My hope is that by the end of these two books, you will have learned the commonly used skills in guitar. Now you may ask, why "with hymns"? To answer that question, let's go back to when I was just learning.

When I was first learning guitar, I simply could not find good, Christian based, learning materials. I did not want to learn guitar and have to fill my time learning secular rock, blues, or jazz (stuff I would never use). I simply wanted to be able to play guitar, and play really good. Solving that problem is what has brought this book into being. A book that teaches you right, but is free from secular songs, riffs, or progressions! Really, this is the book I wish I had, when I was learning!

Back to the question, why "with hymns"? Hymns are the basic Christian song material. They are simple to understand, most are fairly easy to play, and all are filled with Biblical knowledge and insights. To put it simply, they are the perfect songs to learn from! No time is wasted in learning secular men's songs and no space is used for useless methods of playing. Now I would like to clarify. This book does not use ONLY hymns. I have created lots of simple tunes, and chord progressions to give a deeper understanding of some concepts, to help promote finger flexibility and coordination, and to have things to practice on throughout the beginning stages (a stage when most hymns are a little too complicated).

This book is designed to be used alone as a paper teacher, or as a reference guide to teachers who don't want to use the world's methods to teach an instrument that is not only beautiful, but is a wonderful way to bring glory to our God. This book will teach you the main notes on all six strings, the main chords in guitar, D, C, and G (plus a lesson on other common chords) and multiple different "odd and ins" you will need to play correctly. I focus on simpler hymns, and hymn segments in the beginning and as you progress, move on to the more complicated ones. At the back of the book, there is a practice sheet for each lesson. They will help you to further ground your skills. With that in mind, I hope you enjoy the materials in this book, and enjoy "Learning Guitar with Hymns" as much as I did writing it.

TRISTAN NICAUD

The Design of Your Guitar

Your guitar has many parts, each with its own name. You should study the diagram and description of each to fully understand the workings of your guitar. Also, something to remember is that there is no difference between a nylon, and a steel string guitar when it comes to the structure, or method of playing. The only difference is that each type has a different sound.

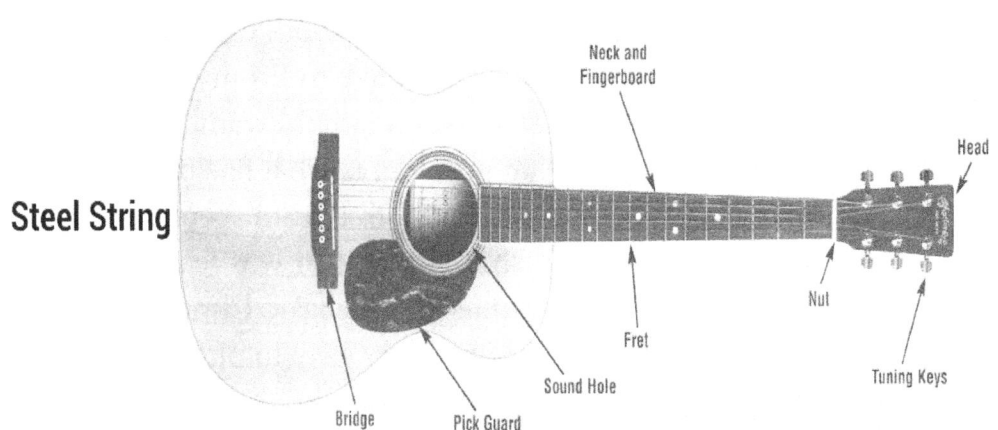

BRIDGE: The bridge is the holding place for the string end which is not tightened. The string ends have a small plastic ball on the steel string guitar, and is manually tied for the nylon stringed guitar.

FRETS: The frets are the lines in between the spaces on the neck. They are one of the most important parts of the guitar.

HEAD: The head holds the other end of the strings and is the spot where you tighten them, which then gives you the different sound for each string. Each string has its own, small "box" which holds the gears for that string. It also is where the maker of your guitar puts their emblem, or name.

NECK AND FINGERBOARD: This is where your left hand fingers will be used (hence the name fingerboard). It is called a neck because it well, looks like a neck!

NUT: This very important piece keeps all the strings from hitting each other and is precisely lined up with bridge. This piece has a designated trench for each string, so when you replace the strings they will tighten in the right way.

PICK GUARD: This part of your guitar protects the body from scratches when the pick go's past the strings. They come in many different styles and designs.

SOUND HOLE: Here is the heart of your guitar! This is the spot where sound comes in, and go's out. It is usually decorated with lines or a design to give it a nice look.

TUNING KEYS: These small knobs are what you turn to tighten your strings. Their sound depends on how much you tighten them. In the diagram, each number represents which string goes to which tuning key, the lowest toned string is "6" and highest toned string is "1" (this is very important to remember for future lessons).

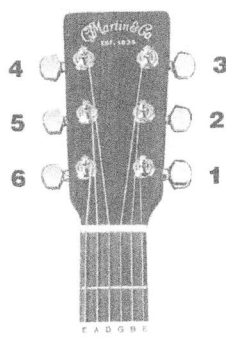

Playing Position

The way that you play guitar is very important, as it can affect your speed, and clearness of tone. There are some vital rules you must follow as you play your guitar.

1. Be relaxed! Do not play in such a way that you have tension on any part of your body.

2. Never tilt the neck in a downward position as this can make it harder to reach the neck (a good guide is to not let the guitar neck go past your elbow).

3. Keep the guitar body straight. Do not tilt the guitar body closer to your stomach so you can see the strings better (it won't take long till you could play blindfolded).

4. Do not squeeze the guitar with your palm.

The below pictures show the correct way to hold a guitar.

                  Sitting down   Standing up

Your upper body position in siting down, and standing should not change much, as the pictures show. If it does, then you will have to adjust each time you play standing, or play sitting. This can cause you to mess up as you won't be comfortable switching from one playing position to another.

Your left hand will be used to finger the strings, and you right hand will strum the strings. The picture at left has a name for each finger used for pressing on the strings. The "number names" are important to remember. Another commonly looked over point is that for the first two to three months your fingers will burn, and have small string indentions in them. This is perfectly normal and expected. You will develop finger flexibility, and hardness the more you play.

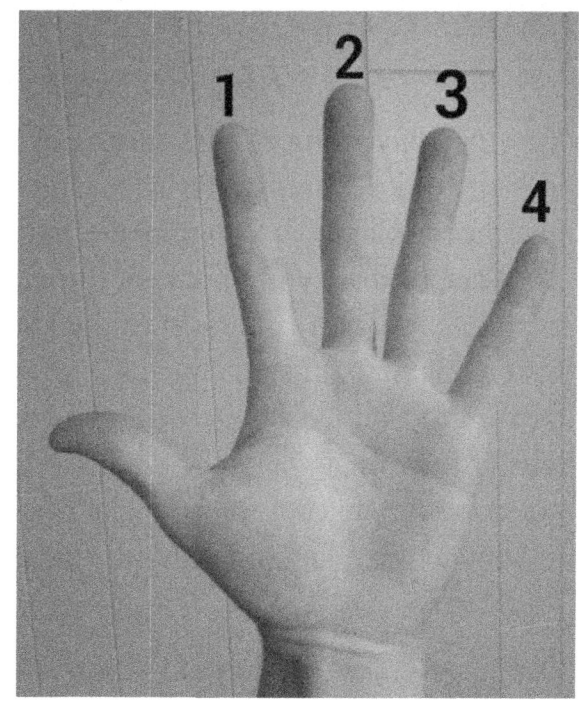

Many people try to say that there is a certain way you must hold your pick. I have seen many different styles and found the best one is..........your own! Hold the pick in the most comfortable manner that has a good grip. Just be careful to not let it fall in the body of your guitar!

The Structure of Guitar Music

You may have noticed the weird looking symbols, numbers, and lines above songs in many older hymnbooks. Those symbols are the very thing that shows the instrument player how to play the music he, or she is playing. Every part and even the place of that symbol is very important to the guitarist. In this section I will explain every part, and most of the symbols that have to do with guitar. You may have noticed that I said "most of the symbols". The reason I am going to explain most of the symbols is because the other ones cannot not be explained until you master these main parts. The other ones are much more complicated, and some are not necessary except for very complicated songs. But regardless of that, future lessons will explain the symbols and what they represent just so you are well rounded.

The first symbol you should know is the staff.

Staff

Around the staff is where you will set the notes, clef symbol, and all the other things that you will need to read notes. It is the main frame of guitar and without it, guitar sheet music would not be impossible.

The staff is made up of lines, and spaces. Within these lines and spaces are where you put the notes.

Lines   **Spaces**

The lines and space are divided into segments which are in between two lines called Bare lines. The area between the Bare lines is called a Measure.

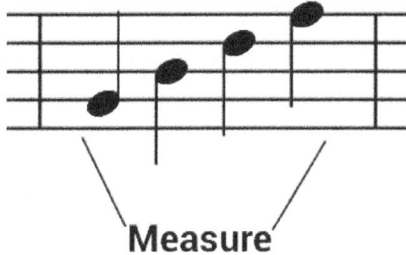

Each measure contains a group of notes. The way you tell what kind of notes you should play is through the Tremble clef, and Time signature.

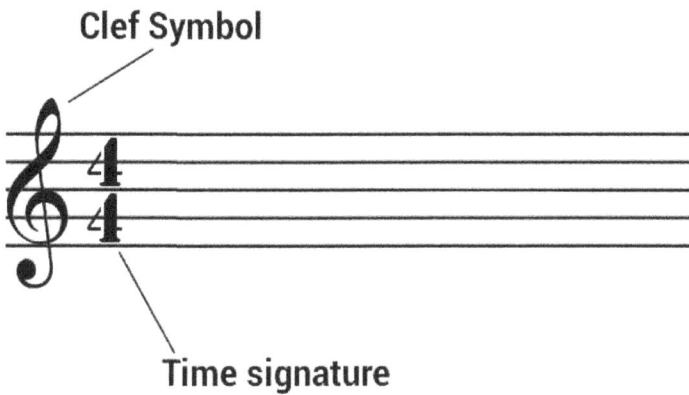

The clef symbol is the symbol that is put before most guitar music sheets. There is one other clef sign for guitar but it is rarely used.
The time signature is what tells you how the notes are played in each song. "How can it do this"? You may ask. Well this brings us to the heart of guitar (and the next section); the notes.

The Notes

The Notes are the letters of guitar. They are what tell you what part of the neck to press on, and for how long. Also, like language, they have their equivalent of commas, periods, and symbols that show you where and how to press on the strings.

This is something I created to help you better understand the notes of guitar. This picture is called a "Note Tree".

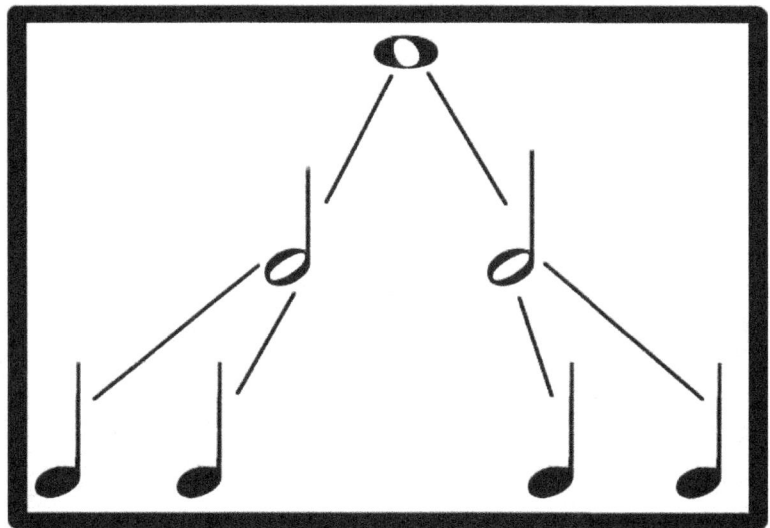

The note at the top is called a "Whole Note".

The notes in the middle are called "Half notes"

The notes at the bottom are call "Quarter Notes.

The note at the top is called a "whole note" because it equals four "beats". A beat is about the same amount it takes you to tap your foot. So, in other words, the "whole note" is the amount of time it takes to tap your foot about four times (try it to get familiar with rhythm). If the whole note equals four beats, then it would make sense that the "half note" equals two beats. Of course, the "quarter notes" equals one beat. For example, if the staff has a whole note then a half note, this means you do not play the half note until the whole note had been plucked for the length of four beats.

When the notes are placed on the staff, and positioned in between the Lines, and Spaces. You get all the different sounds of guitar. Each of those spots on the Lines,

and Spaces represents a certain part of the actual guitar neck. And that is what we will cover in the next sections. I have made a section for each of the strings. So you will cover each string on its own, with a few chord sections in between.
Another thing you will notice is that the most common note used is the quarter note. In your future practice sheets you will see the largest percentage of notes will be quarter notes.

Now it is time to explain the question I presented in the last section. Which was how to understand the Time Signature.

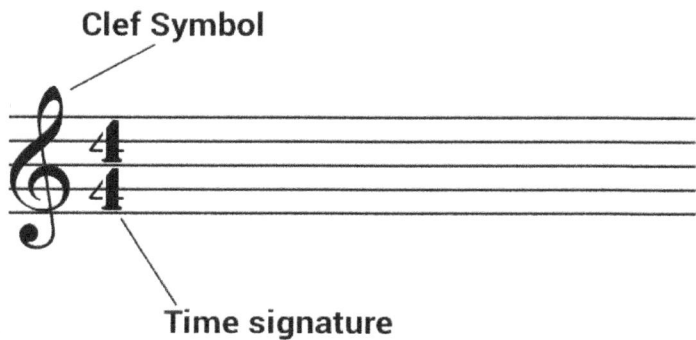

The top note tells you how many beats are in each measure. For example, if the top note is a four, then that means that each measure gets four beats before you move on to the next measure.
The bottom number tells you what note gets one beat. In this example, the quarter note gets one beat. As confusing as it sounds, other notes can also be changed to get one beat, even though it doesn't seem like it can according to the order of notes I discussed previously. Later on I will introduce you to more complicated Time Signatures like 6/8, and 12/8 Time. For the most part though, guitar music is written in 3/4, 2/4, and 4/4 Time.

Notes on the First String

As mentioned before, I have divided the main notes on the guitar by what string they are on. As the title says, in this lesson you will learn the three main notes on the first string.

Before we go to the notes, there is something you might like to see. Each note has a corresponding letter to show where to find that note on a guitar neck. Look at the table below.

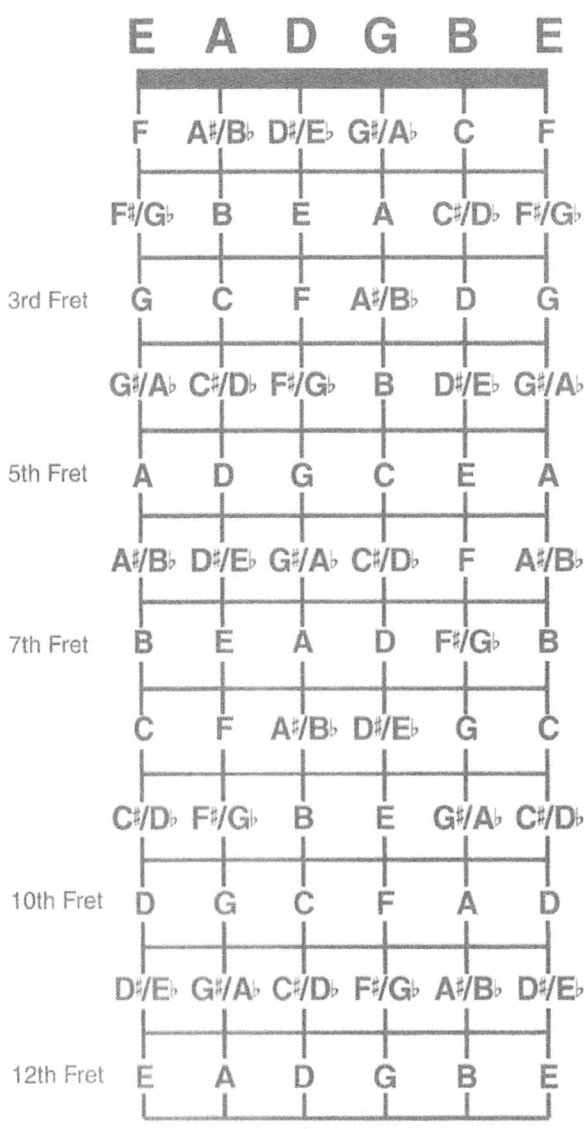

This picture represents every note on the guitar up to the 12th fret (any note above this is not used much). If you may notice that many frets have the same letter in them. This means that if you play those notes, they sound the same (play all of the "G" notes for familiarity). This table is very helpful for those who need to learn how to read notes, you will be referencing it frequently in future lessons.

Now the notes on the first string.

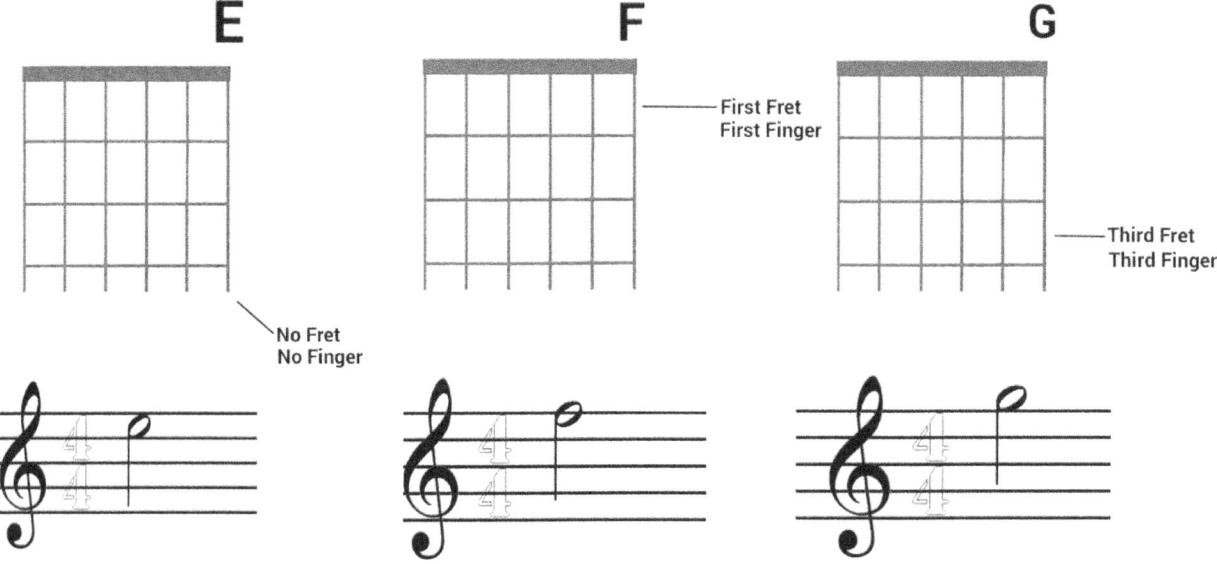

These diagrams represent the three main notes on the first string. The letter will match the diagram, try playing them starting on E and ending on G. Remember to use the correct finger for each fret.

Notes on the Second String

In this lesson you will learn the three main notes on the second string.

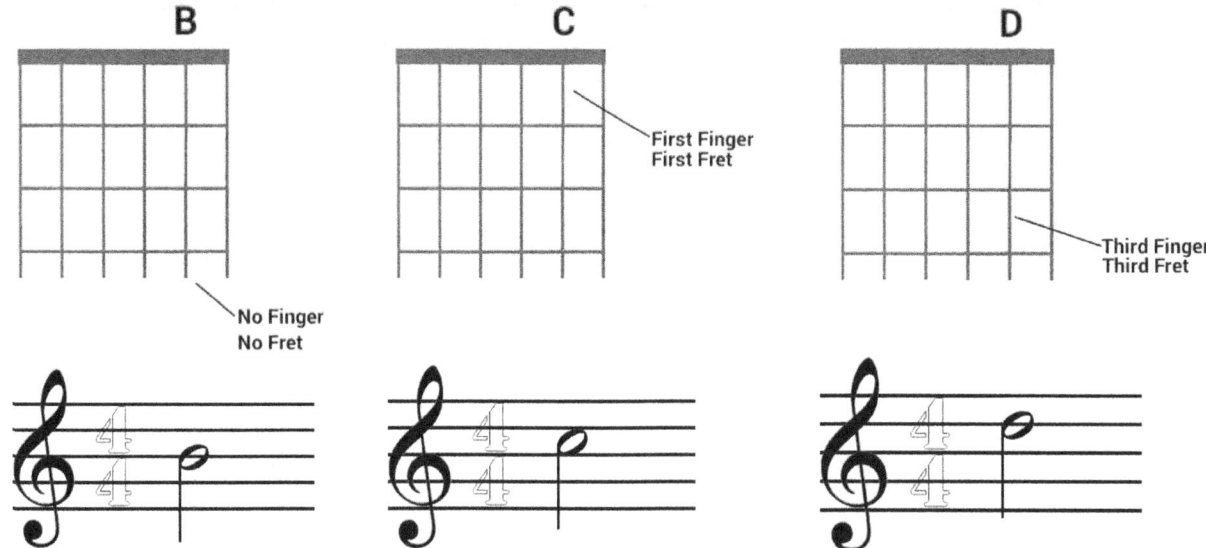

Practice these notes starting with the B, C, and then D, then in reverse. Repeat this about five times. Now practice these simple note progressions. Remember to play with a slow deliberate speed at first, then increase your speed as you gain recognition of the notes.

Do not be concerned if your playing sounds distorted or fuzzy at first. This is expected of a beginner and will disappear in due time. Play the notes below and see if you can guess what tune it is.

If you guessed correctly it was "Joyful Joyful We Adore Thee". This small segment of the song is your beginning fruits of learning guitar. As we progress you will learn many more segments of hymns and, sooner than you think, you will be able to play the full tone of any song!

PS. Always remember to use the practice sheets at the back of the book to further ground your skills.

Notes on the Third String

There are only two main notes on the third string. Nevertheless, they consist of some of the most play notes on the guitar. This is due to the third string being close to the middle of the guitar neck.

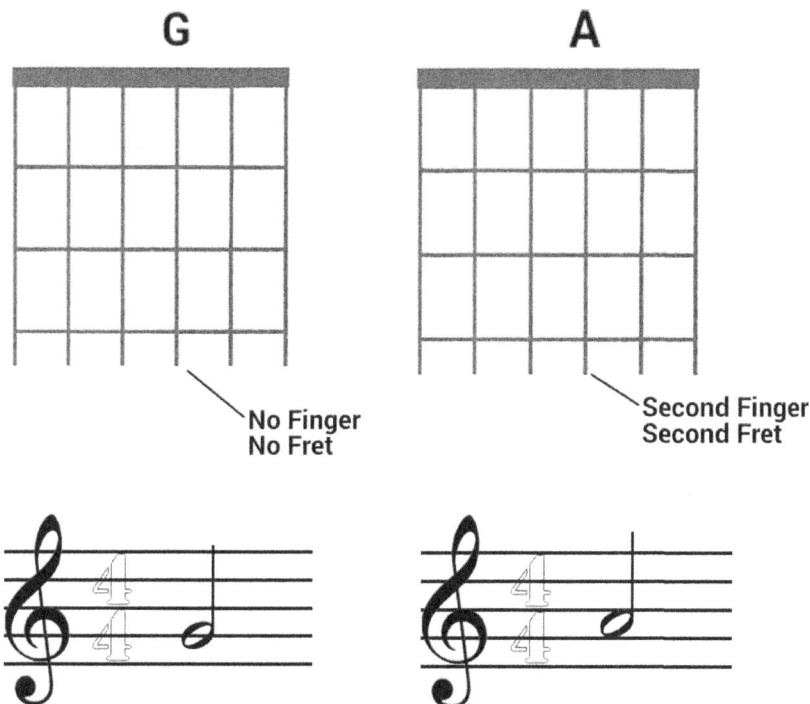

Practice these two notes by playing G and then A. Play it a couple of times, slowly increasing your speed.

Now play this tune.

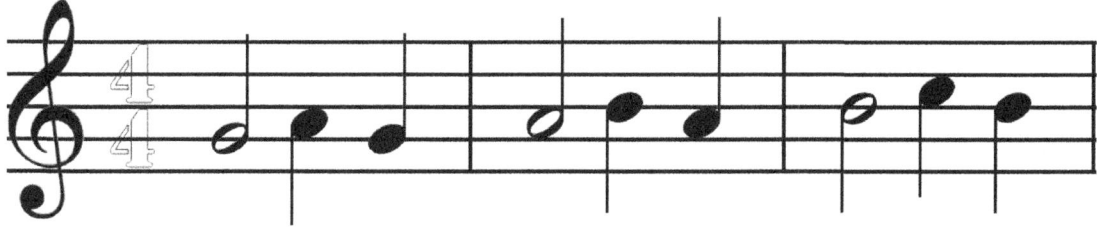

You have now have reached a very important part of learning guitar. You now know all the notes on one octave. What is an octave? To answer that question play the notes below.

You just played all the notes that you learned so far. Now play the bottom note (G) and then play the top (also a G). Do they sound the same? The reason they do is because they are the same, just a higher tone! That is an octave. This concept is the same as the diagram of all the frets in lesson 1. All the letters that are the same sound the same just higher or lower than each other.

Notes on the Fourth String

In this lesson you will learn the three main notes on the fourth string.

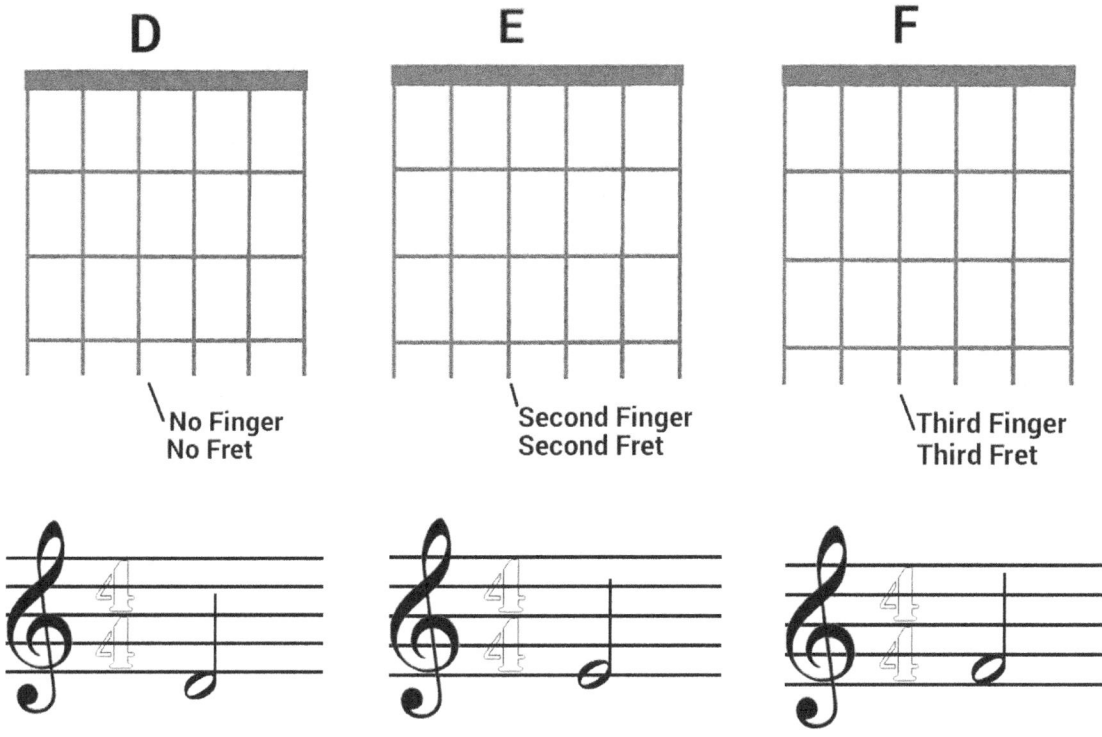

As you may have noticed, these notes are all ones you have played before. The only difference is how deep their tone is. This is important to remember as once you learn the sounds of a "letter" you can distinguish that sound anywhere in the fret board. Play the notes starting at D and going to F and going to back to D. Do this about 5 times saying the names of the notes as you pluck the string.

Now practice this song.

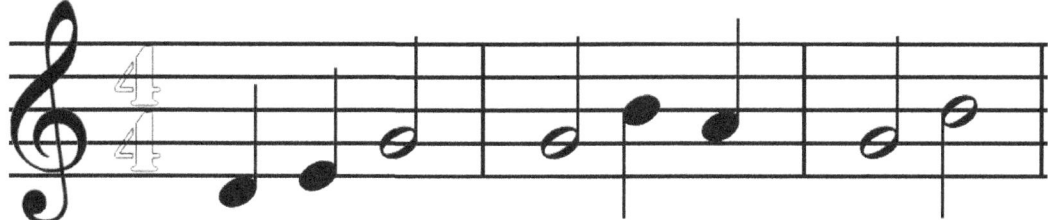

Recognize the tune? "Will the Circle Be Unbroken" is the tune you just played! This song has the notes from all of the strings you know except the first string. Continue to practice these notes and play this song a few more times. This will prepare you to do the practice sheet.

The Chord "D"

So far, you have only learned notes. As you may know, that is not what you usually play in most settings. You play chords. Chords are essentially two or more notes played at the same time. Most chords use strings higher than the third string but, there are many that only use the first three. The chord below is one of the most common chords you will play.

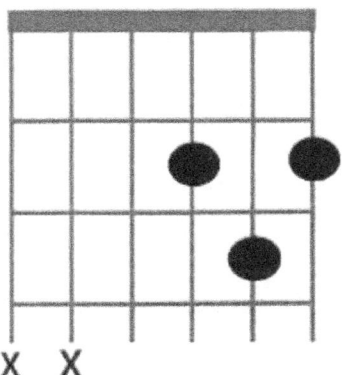

D CHORD

This chord is made up of the notes (in order starting from the fourth string) D, A, D, & G Sharp/F Flat. The two strings with a X on them means don't strum that string. To play this chord, do not press on the first D. Press on the A with your first finger (see lesson 2 for clarity). Press on the second D with your 3 finger, and the G sharp/F flat with your second finger. Practice this chord multiple times and try picking each note individually.

Another thing that is good to know is something called a tie. This means that the first note holds the value of both notes. So when the first note is struck, it is the only one that is played.

Notes on the Fifth String

Now that you have learned your first chord, we will move on to the fifth string. Being the second deepest string, you will now be able to have a larger range of sounds by the end of this lesson.

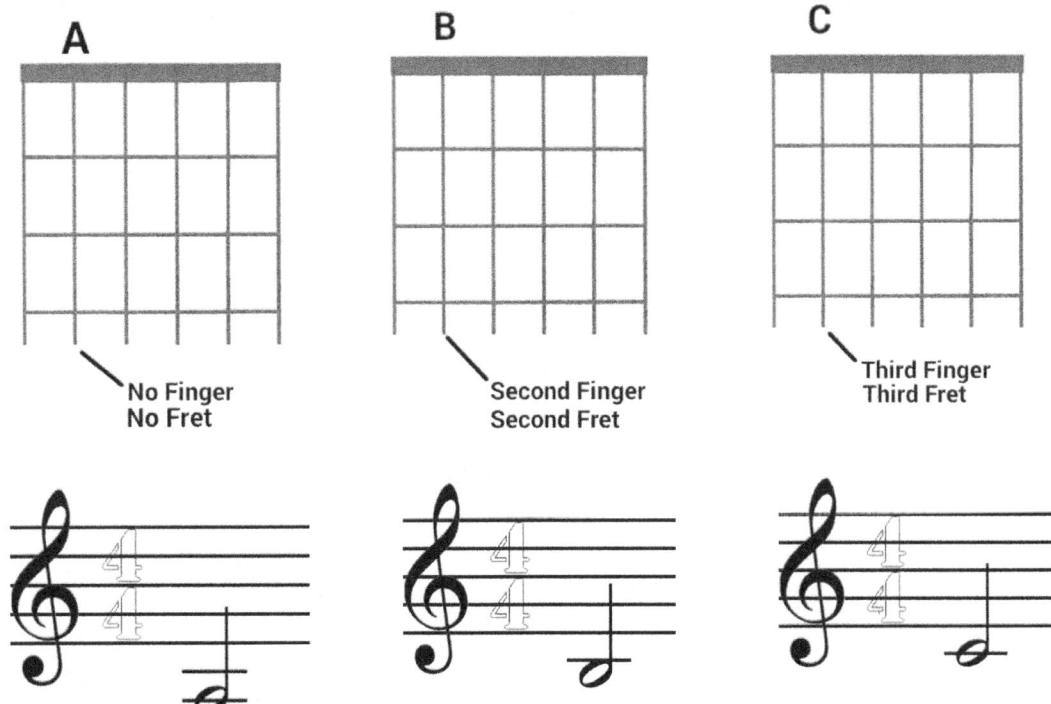

This is a funny string. The names of the main chords are ABC, so it shouldn't be that hard to remember! Play each of these notes twice. Afterwards, play each of them one more time (starting with A) while saying the name of the note.

Now play this song…………

Joshua Fought the Battle of Jericho

Play this song a couple of times. Attempt to play faster with each try to gain greater control over your fingers. As always, don't forget to do the practice sheet!

The Chord "C"

This chord is commonly used in hymns. It is important to learn it early on so you will be able to play songs well.

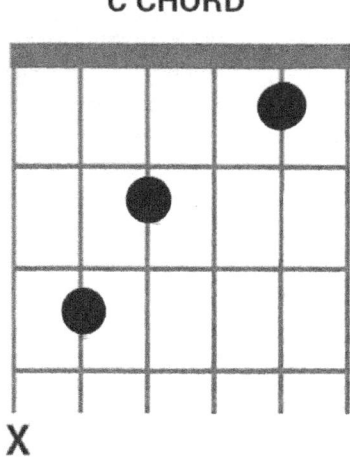

The notes for this chord are (deepest to highest) C, E, G, C, and F. Press on the lower C with your third finger. Press on E with your second finger, and the higher C with your first finger. Play firmly and steady remembering to not press on the sixth string. As a reminder, the lower and higher sound will sound the same. Another thing that you have to learn is "steps". A whole step is the distance between three frets, and a half step is the distance between two frets.

This is very important to know when you learn about sharps and flats, and scales.

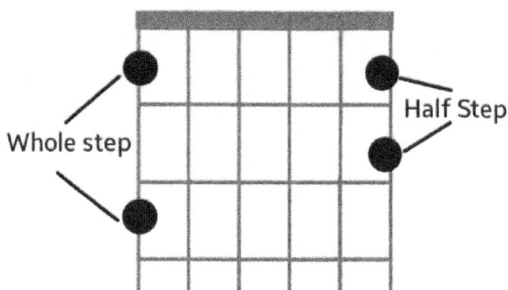

Notes on the Sixth string

You have reached the last string! This string is the same as most of the other strings, having three main notes.

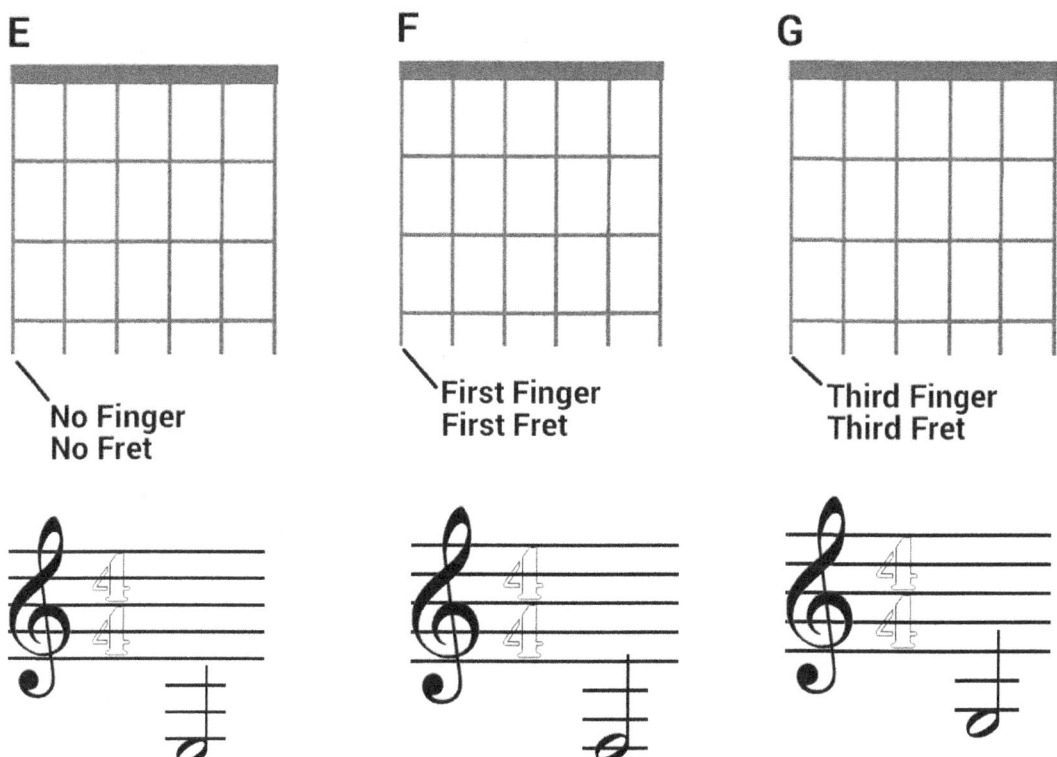

Play each of these strings twice starting with the lowest string. This chapter concludes the main notes are all the strings. Remember though, these are just the main notes. You may have notice that we have not covered every fret. The reason for this is that those frets are essentially halfway notes. They do have a letter applied to them, and they also have note symbol. They are simply more complicated to understand, so they need their own lesson. They will be covered in book 2, but for now, continue to practice the notes and chords you have learned. Always remember to do the practice sheets.

The Chord "G"

This is one of the most common chords you will play. Used in hymns and folk songs quite often, it is a very important chord.

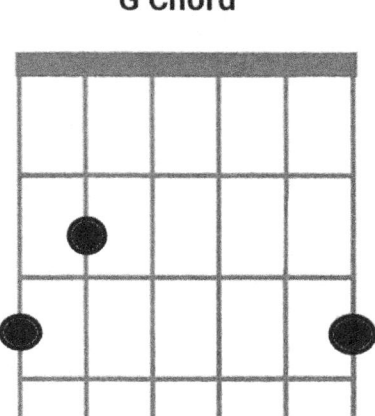

This chord is made up the notes (from deepest to highest) G, B, D, G, B, and G. It is played by pressing on the deepest G with your second finger, deepest B with your first finger, and the highest G with you third finger. Strum with a steady downward stroke. Don't press to hard with your pick.

Also, some more symbols you need to know are called "rests". Look at the pictures below.

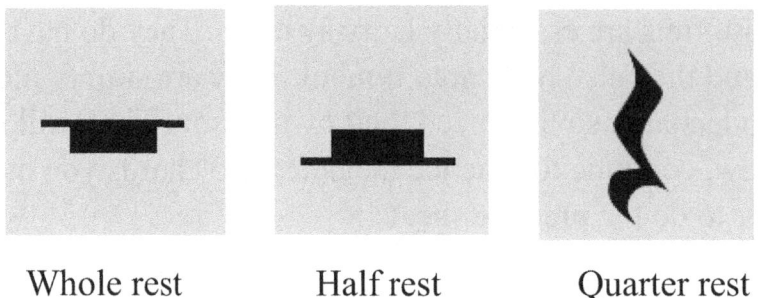

A rest is a pause in music where you do not play a note. When one of these rest are positioned on the staff, you pause from playing for the length of it corresponding note (a half rest means you pause for the length of a half note). See the practice sheet for some notes with rests mixed in.

Common Chords

In this lesson you are going to learn about some common chords played in many different songs.

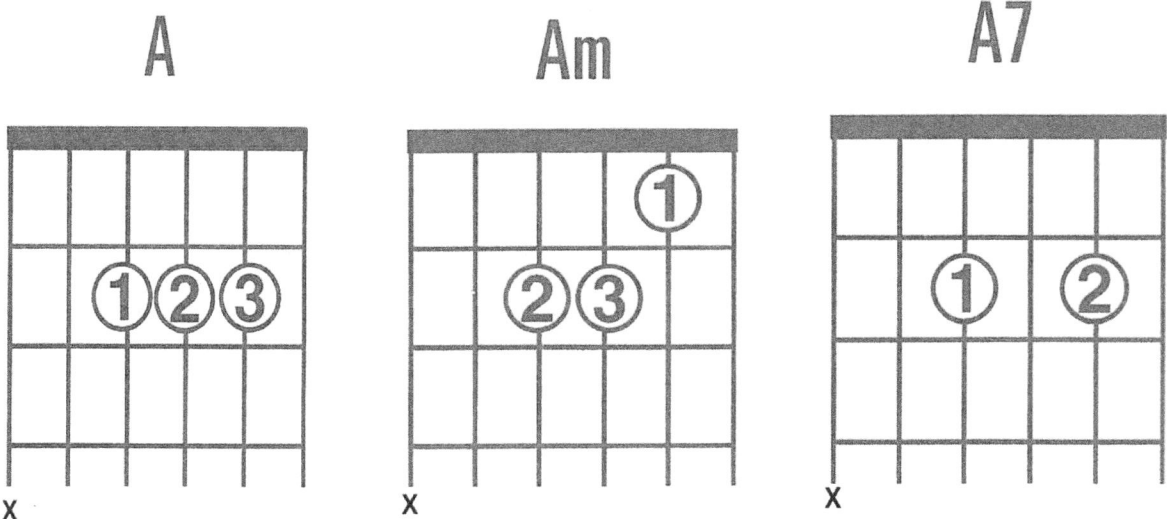

These chords have a mellow tone, and are used in nearly every genre of music.

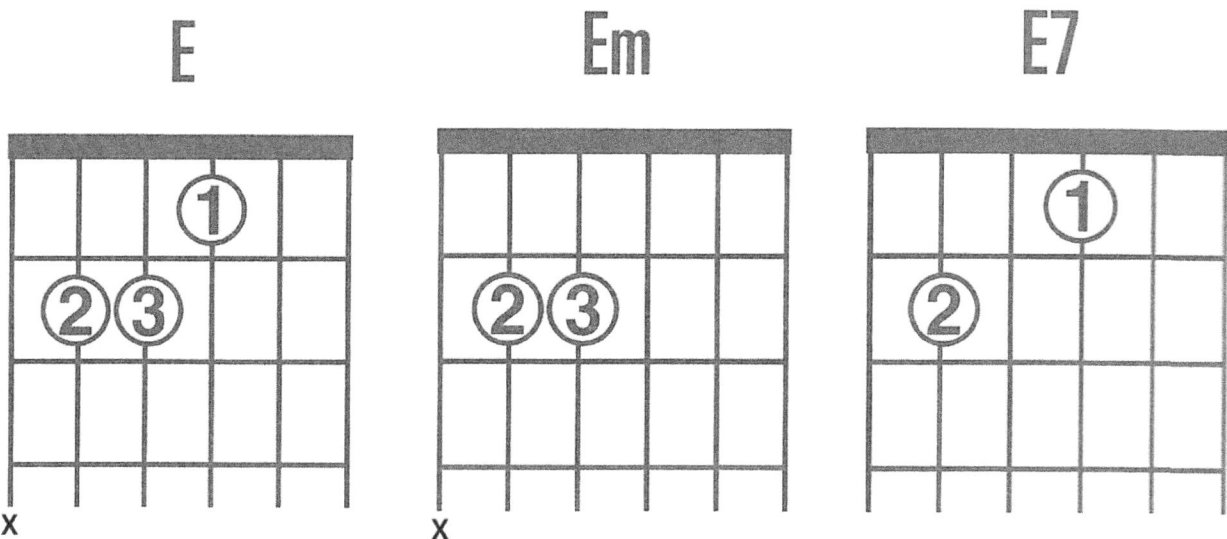

These chords have deep sounding tones and are used very often as well. Play each chord a couple of times, and then do the practice sheet.

Practice Sheets

Practice sheet for

"The design of your Guitar."

1. Put the correct letter in the blanks for the below picture.

A. Bridge

B. Frets

C. Head

D. Neck and fingerboard

E. Nut

F. Pick guard

G. Sound hole

H. Tuning keys

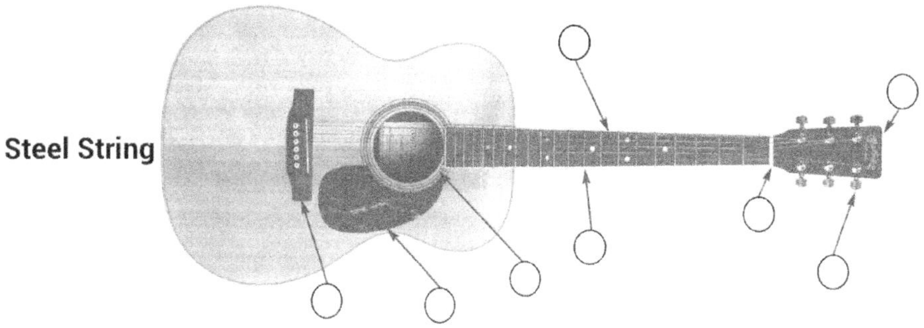

2. Describe the function of each of the Guitar's main parts.

Bridge:

_____
_____
_____.

Frets:

_____
_____
_____.

Head:

_____
_____
_____.

Neck and fingerboard:

_____
_____.

Nut:

_____
_____
_____.

Pick guard:

_____
_____
_____.

Sound hole:

_____
_____
_____.

Tuning keys:

_____
_____
_____.

3. What are Frets?

_____.

Practice sheet for
"Playing Position"

True or False.

1. It is good to squeeze the guitar neck when playing.
   _____.

2. Be relaxed when you are playing.
   _____.

3. Fill in the blanks below.

When you are playing the guitar, you should play in a _____ manner. Never _____ the guitar neck. Your _____ hand will finger the strings and your _____ hand will strum the strings. Your body position should _____ as you play. Always remember to not let your _____ fall in the body of your guitar.

Practice sheet for

"The Structure of Guitar Music"

Draw a line from each word to the correct picture.

A. Staff

B. Lines

C. Spaces

D. Bare Lines

E. Measure

F. Clef Symbol & Time Signature

2. Describe the function of each word below.

Staff:

_____

_____.

30

Lines:
_____
_____

Spaces:
_____
_____

Bare Lines:
_____
_____

Measure:
_____
_____

Clef Symbol & Time Signature:
_____
_____

Practice sheet for
"The Notes"

1. Name the kind of note in each picture below.

_____.

_____.

_____.

2. What does a "Beat" mean?

_____

_____.

3. In the picture below, explain what each word means.

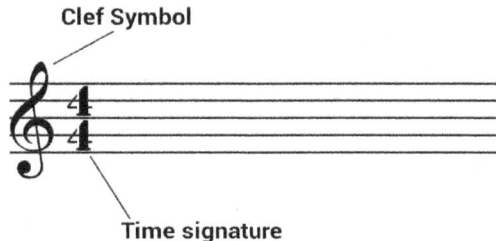

Clef Symbol:

_____.

Time Signature:

_____.

Practice sheet for
"Notes on the First String"

1. Draw a line from the correct picture too it's corresponding note.

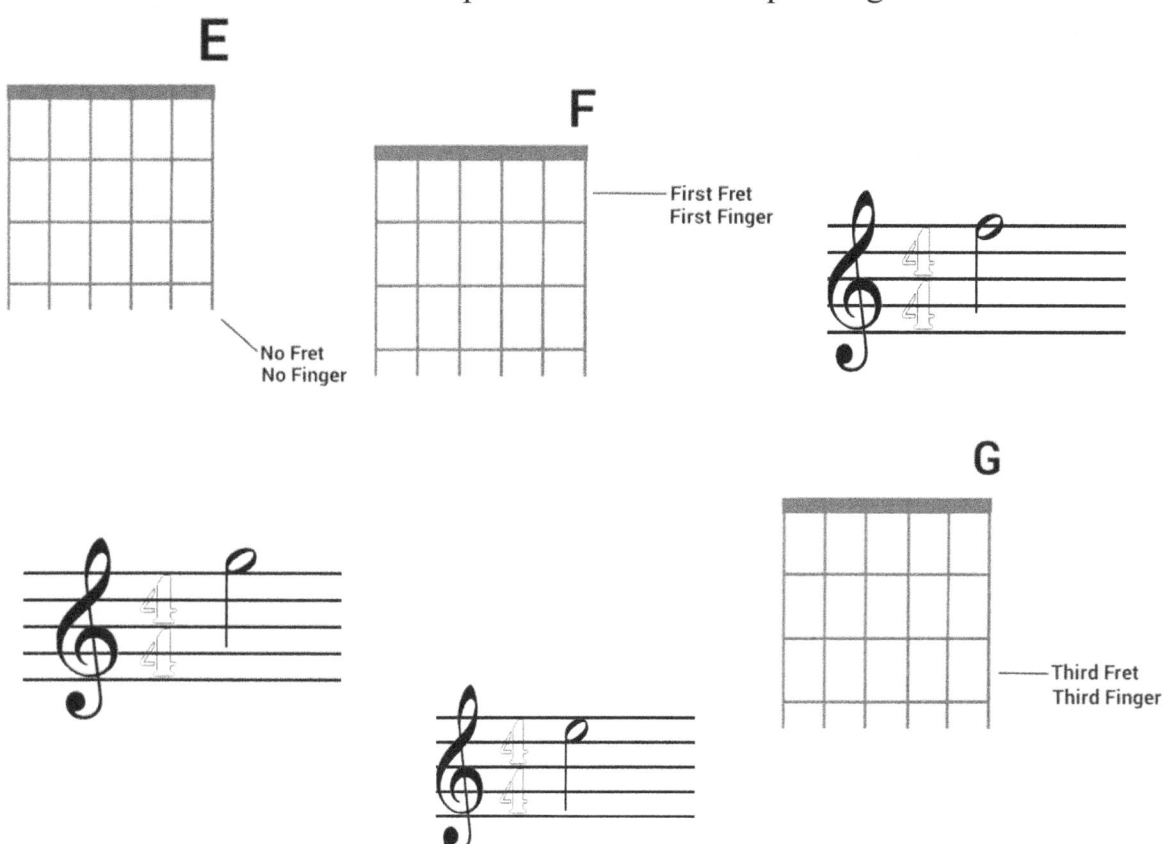

2. Draw a shape around each letter using the shape key below.

G. Square

A. Triangle

D. Circle

B. Rectangle

E. Diamond

C. Pentagon

F. Oval

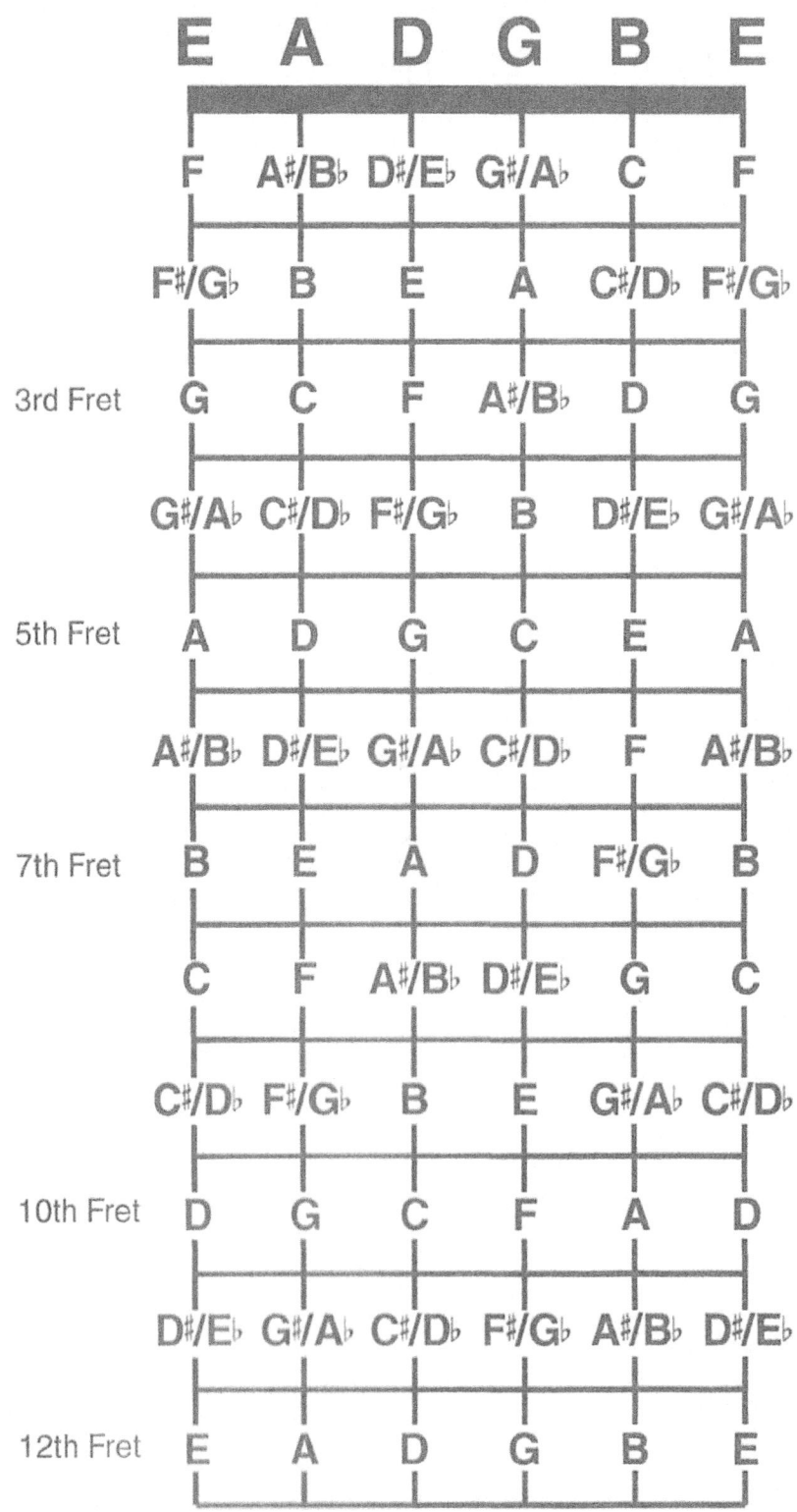

Practice the notes below.

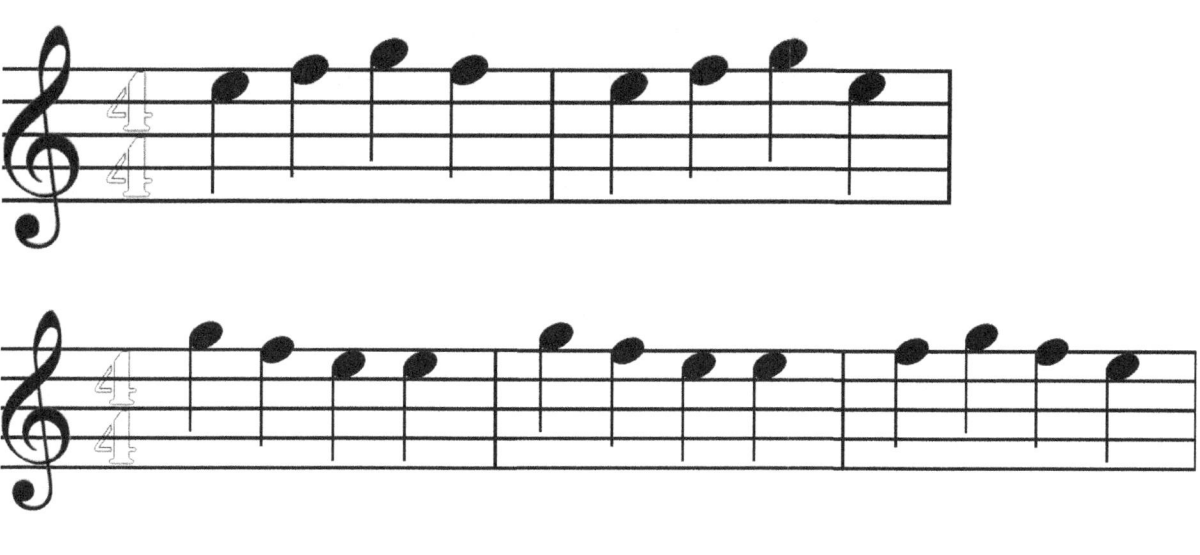

Practice sheet for
"Notes on the second string"

1. Draw a line from the correct picture too it's corresponding note.

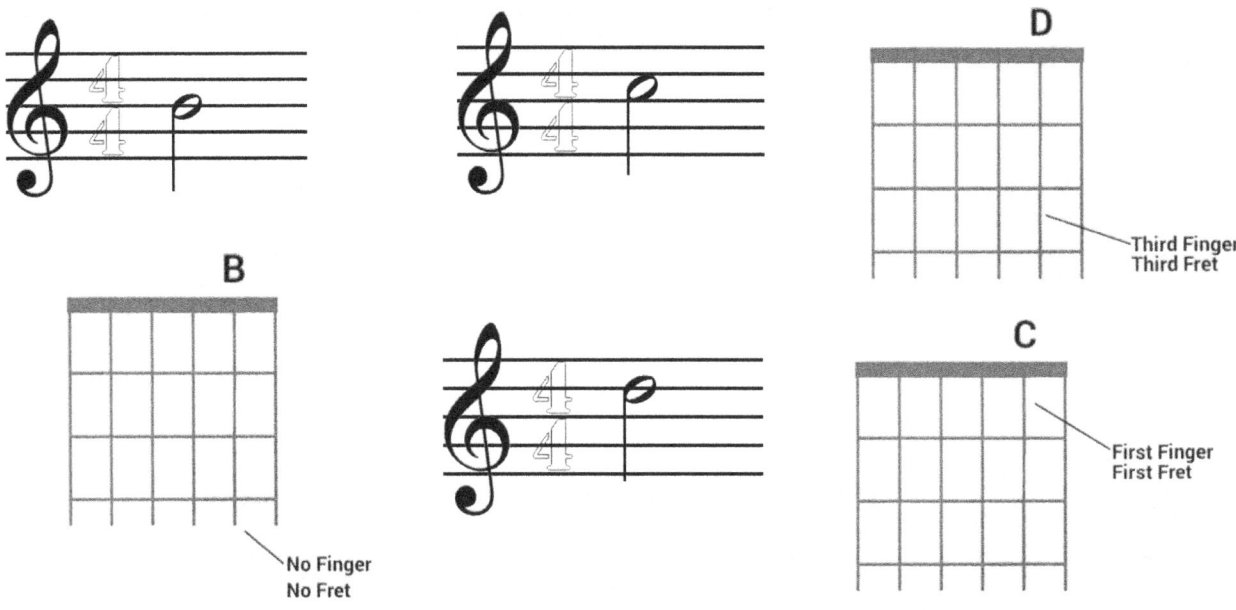

2. Play the tone below with special attention paid to the timing.

Practice sheet for

"Notes on the Third String"

1. Match the correct note to it's correct diagram (there is an extra note).

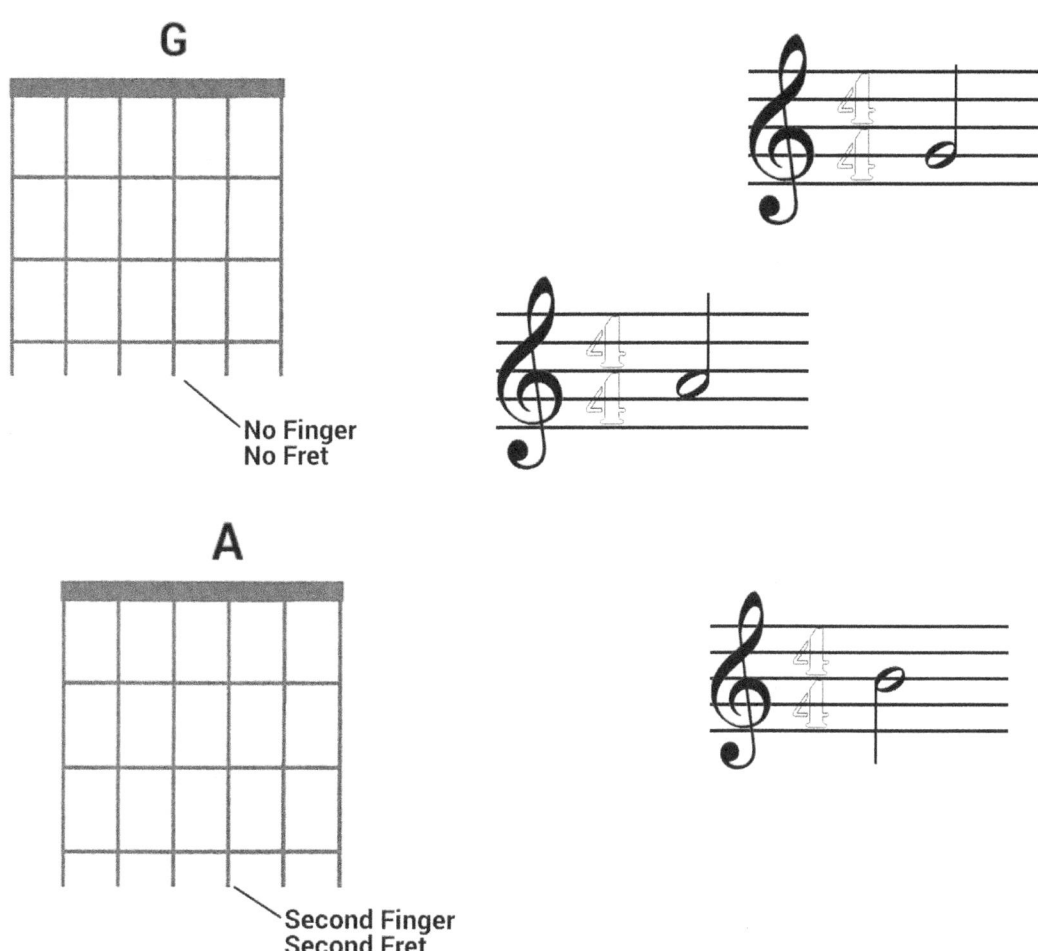

2. What is an octave?

_____
_____

Practice sheet for
"Notes on the Fourth String"

1. Draw a line from each picture too it's corresponding note.

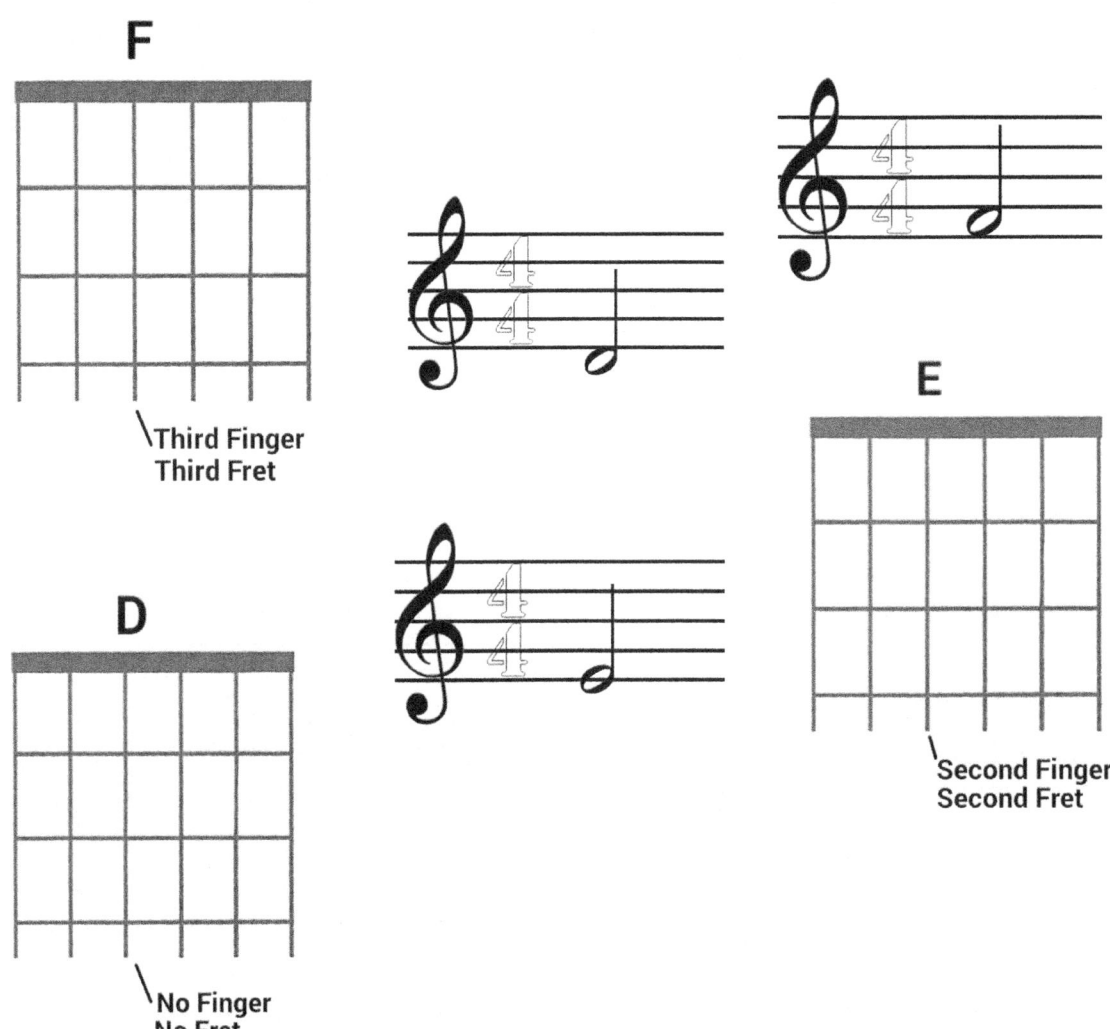

2. Play the song below

Practice sheet for
"The Chord D"

1. Play the D chord multiple times, slowly at first, and then increasing your speed. Make sure you continue to press on the strings throughout the strumming.

2, Play the chords below. Strum once for each time D is shown.

40

Practice sheet for
"Notes on the Fifth String"

1. Match each note to it's diagram.

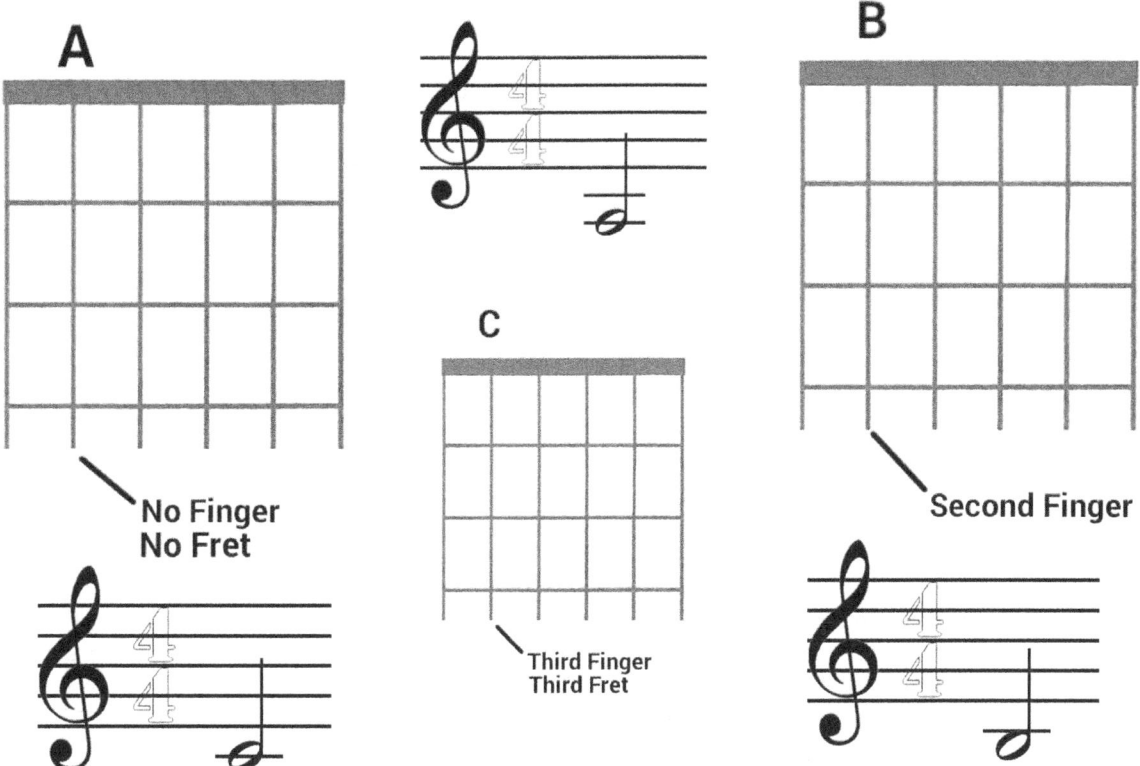

2. What is the order of the notes on the Fifth String?

A. CBA

B. ABC

Ç. CAB

D. BAC

Practice sheet for
"The Chord C"

1. In this practice sheet, you will combine the two chords you have learned so far. Play slowly as you change to the next chord. Remember speed is not nearly as important as clarity.

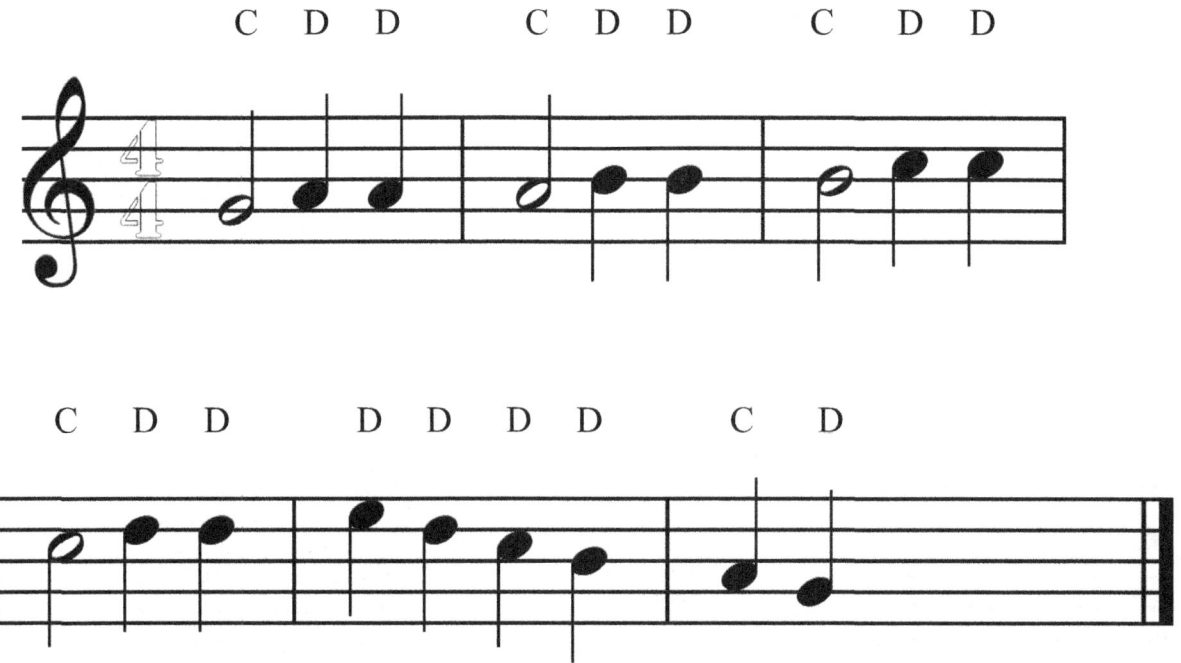

Practice sheet for
"Notes on the Sixth String"

1. Play the tune below.

2. Match the correct note to its picture

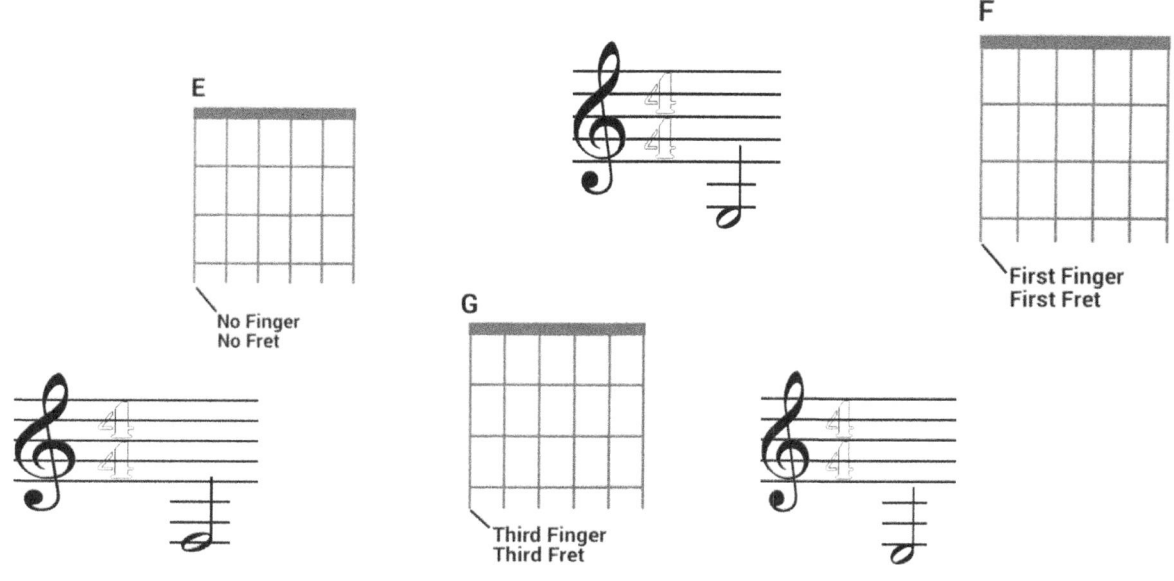

43

Practice sheet for
"The Chord G"

1. Practice the strum pattern below

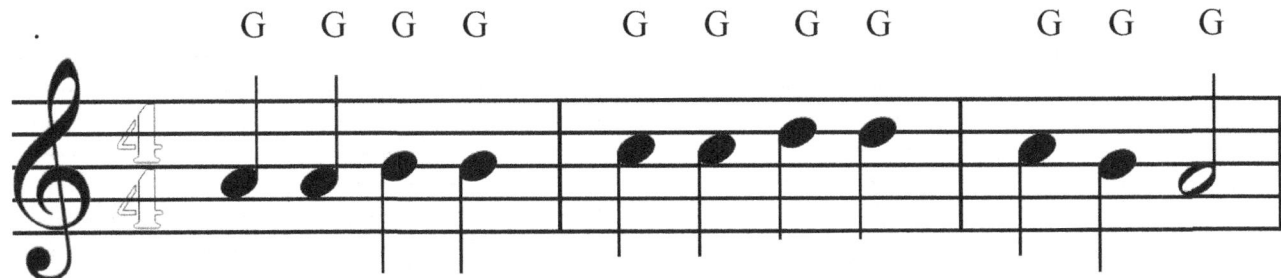

2. Play the notes below. Remember to pause at each rest.

Practice sheet for
"Common Chords"

1. Draw a line from each chord to it's name.

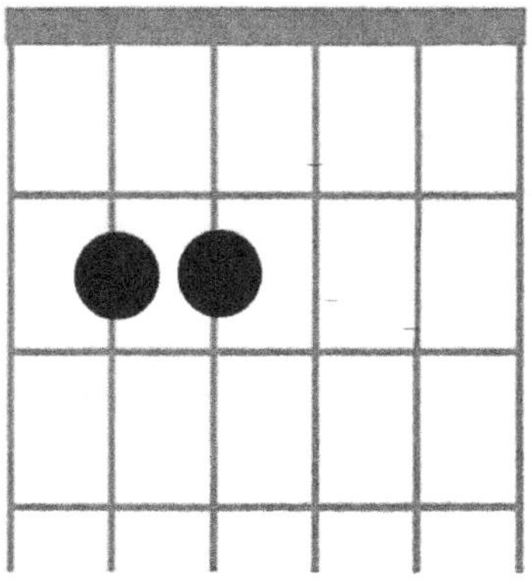

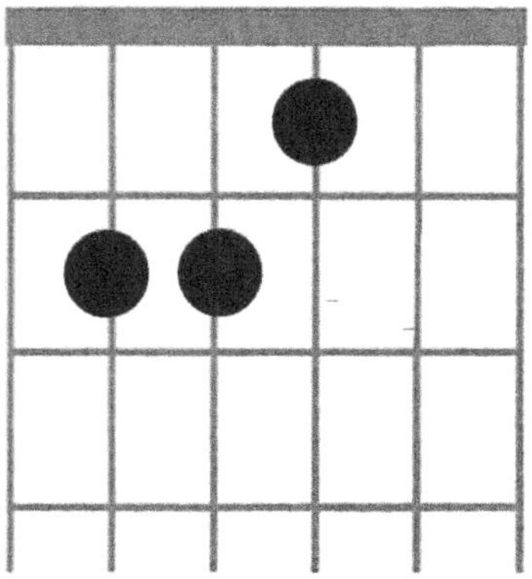

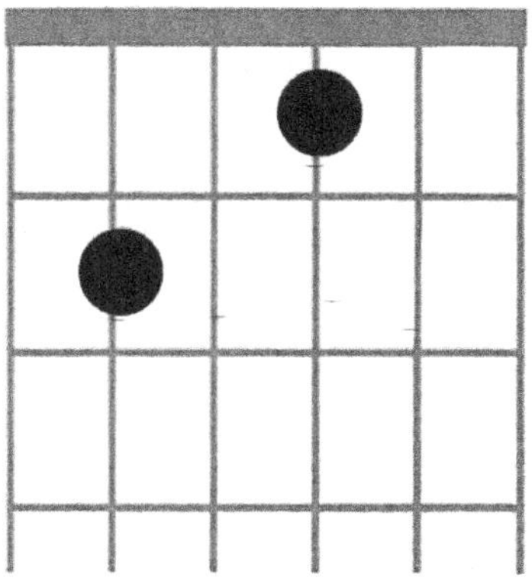

E

Em

E7

A

Am

A7

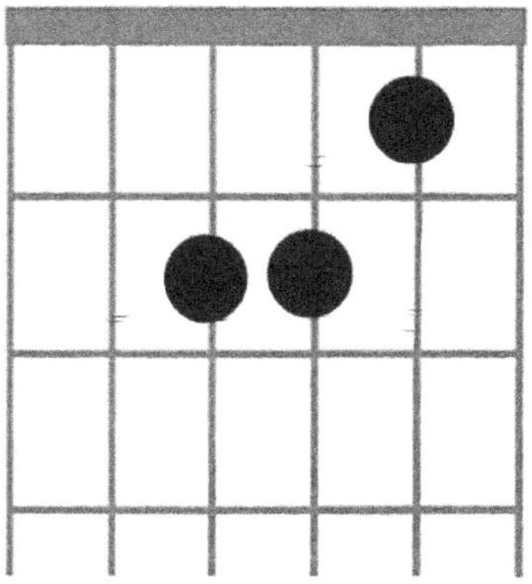

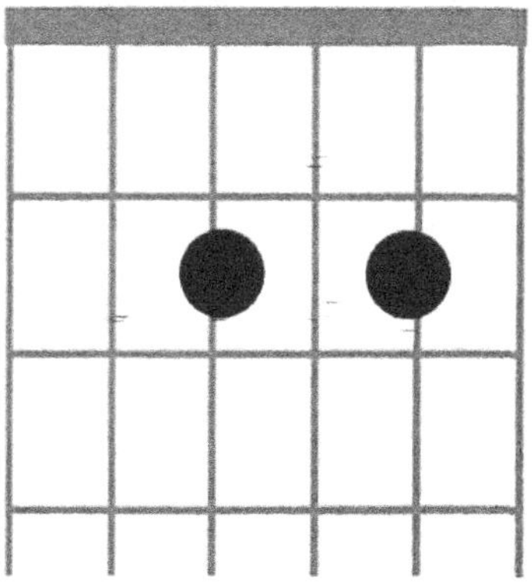

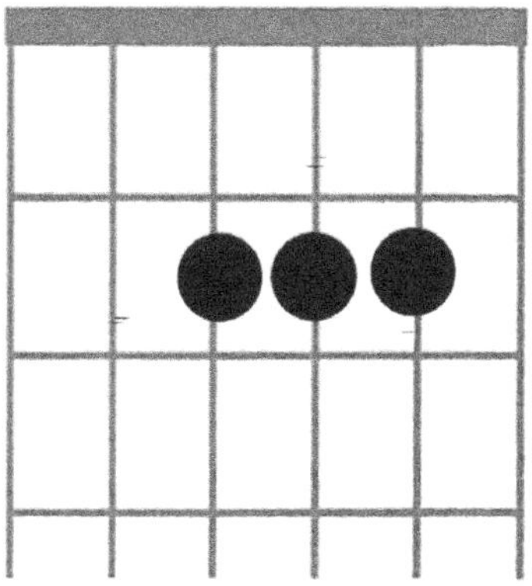

45

2. Play the chord progression below. The notes are there so you can keep time, there is no need to play them.

| E | Em | E7 E |

| A | Am | A7 |

| D G | C E | A7 D |

I'm done…………Now what?

Awesome! Although I hope you don't stop here. To further your studies, I suggest getting book 2 in the "Learning Guitar with Hymns" series. In it, you will learn a whole bunch more stuff. Such as eighth notes, sixteenth notes, articulation, fingerstyle, bass strumming, sharps and flats, and Travis picking.

Hope to teach you again soon!

Tristan Nicaud

The material in this book is for personal, or teaching use. The majority of the diagrams, and drawings are the original work of the author, and cannot be copied in any form.

Made in United States
North Haven, CT
17 June 2023

37873122R00026